A TRUE BOOK

The Presidency

CHRISTINE TAYLOR-BUTLER

Children's Press®
A Division of Scholastic Inc.
New York   Toronto   London   Auckland   Sydney
Mexico City   New Delhi   Hong Kong
Danbury, Connecticut

Content Consultant

David R. Smith, PhD

Academic Adviser and

Adjunct Assistant Professor of History

University of Michigan–Ann Arbor

Reading Consultant

Cecilia Minden-Cupp, PhD

Early Literacy Consultant and Author

Library of Congress Cataloging-in-Publication Data

Taylor-Butler, Christine.
The Presidency / by Christine Taylor-Butler.
   p. cm.—(A true book)
Includes bibliographical references and index.
ISBN-13: 978-0-531-12634-9 (lib. bdg.)   978-0-531-14784-9 (pbk.)
ISBN-10: 0-531-12634-X (lib. bdg.)   0-531-14784-3 (pbk.)
1. Presidents—United States—Juvenile literature. 2.
Presidents—United States—History—Juvenile literature. I. Title. II. Series.
JK517.T395 2008
973.09'9—dc22   2007012256

All rights reserved. Published in 2008 by Children's Press, an imprint of Scholastic Inc.
Published simultaneously in Canada. Printed in the United States of America.
SCHOLASTIC, CHILDREN'S PRESS, A TRUE BOOK, and associated logos are trademarks and/or registered trademarks of Scholastic Inc.
1 2 3 4 5 6 7 8 9 10 R 17 16 15 14 13 12 11 10 09

Find the Truth!

Everything you are about to read is true *except* for one of the sentences on this page.

Which one is **TRUE**?

T or F George Washington got paid nothing for being president.

T or F The Constitution gives the president unlimited power.

Find the answer in this book.

We the People *...*

Article 1

Contents

THE **BIG** TRUTH!

1600 Pennsylvania Avenue

4

Abraham Lincoln hid his
speeches in his top hat.

In this engraving, George Washington takes the oath of office as the first president of the United States. The date was April 30, 1789.

CHAPTER 1

Who Can Be President?

The first president was elected in 1789—2 years after the Constitution was written.

Do you know that most adult American citizens can become president of the United States? There are three requirements. The person must have been born in the United States. He or she has to be at least 35 years old. And a president must have lived in the United States for at least 14 years.

The president's office is called the Oval Office. The walls of this room are curved.

One Job, Many Duties

Once he or she takes office, the president is in charge of the country's relations with the rest of the world. The president leads the people when disasters occur. He or she heads the military. The president also makes sure the laws of the United States Constitution are followed. The Constitution is the document that created our government. It is the highest law in the country.

Being president is a challenge, but the job pays well. The president earns $400,000 per year. He or she also receives $50,000 for office expenses and another $100,000 for travel. And the president gets to live in the house shown below!

The White House is where presidents have lived and worked since 1800.

This photo is of Grover Cleveland during his inauguration in 1885. During the inauguration ceremony, a new president takes the oath of office.

CHAPTER 2

The Presidency

The oath of office is in the Constitution: Article II, Section 1. Look it up!

The first thing every president does is take an **oath of office**. The new president promises to do the best job possible for the United States. This takes place during a formal ceremony called an **inauguration**. It is held on January 20, two and a half months after an election. The president serves a four-year **term** and could serve for one more term of office after that.

Henry Kissinger (left), secretary of state under President Nixon, with Pham Dang Lam during their 1972 talks to end the Vietnam War.

Many Hats, Many Hands

The president makes sure the nation's laws are followed. He or she also has the power to approve or block new laws made by Congress. If the president doesn't like a law, he or she can **veto** it. Congress can still pass a law after a president's veto. But two-thirds of the Congress must vote to do so.

The president has **cabinet** officers who give advice and also help run the **executive** branch. The president chooses cabinet members, but they must be confirmed by the Senate.

The president sets **foreign policy**. He or she is also in charge of the army, navy, and other branches of the military.

The president also appoints judges for the **federal**, or national, courts. These include the justices of the Supreme Court, the highest court in the land. The decisions of the Supreme Court affect the rights of all citizens. Supreme Court justices can keep their jobs for the rest of their lives.

President Reagan appointed Sandra Day O'Connor to be the first ➡ woman Supreme Court justice.

On August 8, 1974, President Richard Nixon resigned from office. Newspapers reported his decision before he made his televised announcement to the American people that night.

Impeachment

The president is powerful. But the law is more powerful. Congress can **impeach**, or accuse a president of committing a crime. The House of Representatives makes the accusation. The Senate then holds a trial. The president is removed from office if two-thirds of the senators vote him or her guilty.

Only two presidents have been impeached: Andrew Johnson and Bill Clinton. The Senate did not find either one guilty. Richard Nixon resigned when it looked as if he would be impeached.

Who Takes Over?

What happens if a president dies or leaves office? The vice president takes over. What if something happens to the vice president, and so on? President Harry Truman signed the Presidential Succession Act in 1947. This law answers that question.

The "order of succession" list is 18 people long. Here are the first five.

1. Vice president
2. Speaker of the House
3. President pro tempore of the Senate*
4. Secretary of state
5. Secretary of the treasury

*This person is elected by members of the Senate.

On November 22, 1963, President John F. Kennedy was assassinated. Vice President Lyndon B. Johnson was sworn in two hours later aboard the president's airplane, Air Force One.

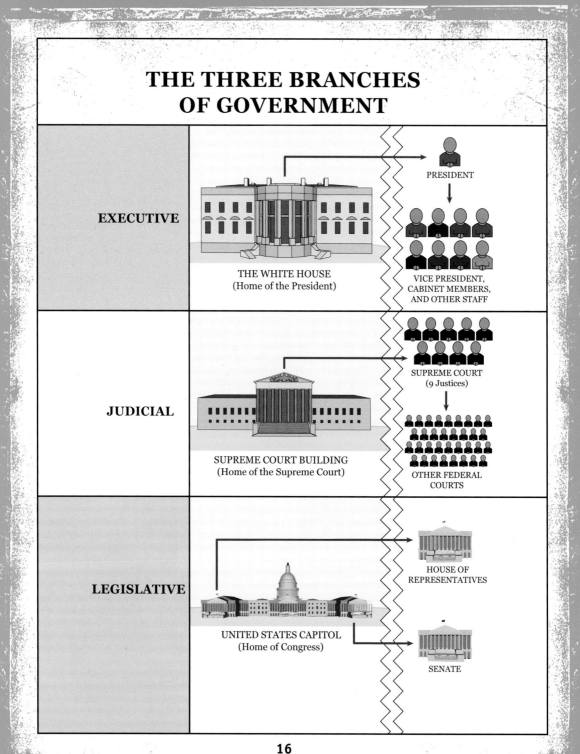

THE THREE BRANCHES OF GOVERNMENT

EXECUTIVE

THE WHITE HOUSE
(Home of the President)

PRESIDENT

VICE PRESIDENT,
CABINET MEMBERS,
AND OTHER STAFF

JUDICIAL

SUPREME COURT BUILDING
(Home of the Supreme Court)

SUPREME COURT
(9 Justices)

OTHER FEDERAL
COURTS

LEGISLATIVE

UNITED STATES CAPITOL
(Home of Congress)

HOUSE OF
REPRESENTATIVES

SENATE

CHAPTER 3

The Executive Branch

About 2% of all U.S. employees work for the executive branch of government.

There are three branches of the U.S. government: the executive branch, the legislative branch, and the judicial branch. Each branch helps control the power of the other two so no one branch becomes too powerful. This system is called checks and balances.

Checks and Balances

Here are just a few of the ways the checks and
balances system works.

★ Congress passes a new law. It does not go into
  effect until the president approves it.

★ The president abuses his power and breaks a
  law. Congress impeaches him.

★ A law passed by Congress and approved by
  the president is unfair to a group of Americans.
  The Supreme Court can rule that the new law
  is unconstitutional.

**President Jimmy
Carter exercises his
executive power by
signing a bill into
law. Senators and
representatives
look on.**

33 USA

The Peace Corps

1999

Peace Corps volunteers help train workers in other countries.

The checks and balances are important because running the United States is a huge job with a great deal of power. The president needs help to run the executive branch. The departments and agencies of this branch do many things. Here are a few examples. The Central Intelligence Agency (CIA) collects information about possible threats to the United States. The Peace Corps sends volunteers to help improve lives in poor countries. The job of the Department of Labor is to protect U.S. workers.

CHAPTER 4

The First President

As president, George Washington was offered $25,000 a year.

George Washington was the perfect choice to be the first president of the United States. His army had defeated the British in the **Revolutionary War**. He organized and led the founding fathers in creating the Constitution. He was respected and admired by almost every American.

Today, George Washington's presidential salary would be equivalent to more than $500,000. Washington refused his salary because he was already a wealthy man.

George Washington took the oath of office at Federal Hall in New York City.

George Washington left his home in Virginia and traveled for eight days on horseback to take the oath of office. The inauguration took place in New York City on April 30, 1789. Later that day, Washington spoke to Congress. One witness wrote that the new president trembled as he spoke. He knew the importance and difficulty of his job.

Washington's Decisions

Washington realized that he couldn't do all the work alone. He set up the first United States cabinet and appointed four men to these jobs: attorney general, secretary of state, secretary of the treasury, and secretary of war. These cabinet members lead departments that are still part of the executive branch. (The Department of War is now called the Department of Defense.)

Andrew Ellicott was the chief architect for the layout of the country's new capital city, Washington, D.C. This is a map of his design.

Washington selected a site for the new capital city. New York was the nation's first capital, then Philadelphia. The new capital city would be built along the Potomac River starting in 1800. This city is called Washington, D.C., which is short for District of Columbia.

Washington served for two four-year terms. Some people wanted him to serve a third time, but he said no. He wanted to see power transferred to a new president.

Washington asked people to call him Mr. President when they spoke to him. Leaders in almost every other country went by a grand title, such as "Your Majesty." Today, we still say "Mr. President." When a woman is elected president, she'll be called "Madame President."

1600 Pennsylvania

Have you heard that address before? It is the address of the White House in Washington, D.C., where the president lives and works. It has 132 rooms, including 3 kitchens and 35 bathrooms.

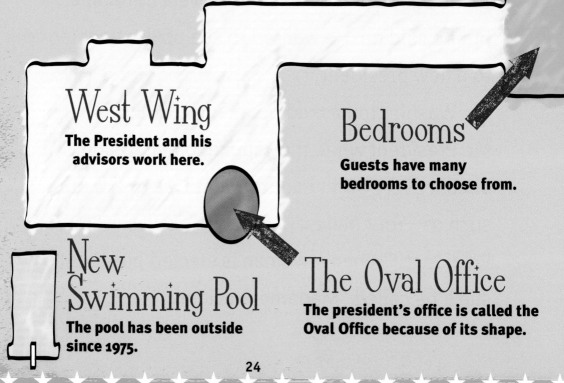

Dining Room

Presidents, queens, and other guests eat here.

Kitchen

Chefs can cook snacks for 1,000 people.

West Wing

The President and his advisors work here.

Bedrooms

Guests have many bedrooms to choose from.

New Swimming Pool

The pool has been outside since 1975.

The Oval Office

The president's office is called the Oval Office because of its shape.

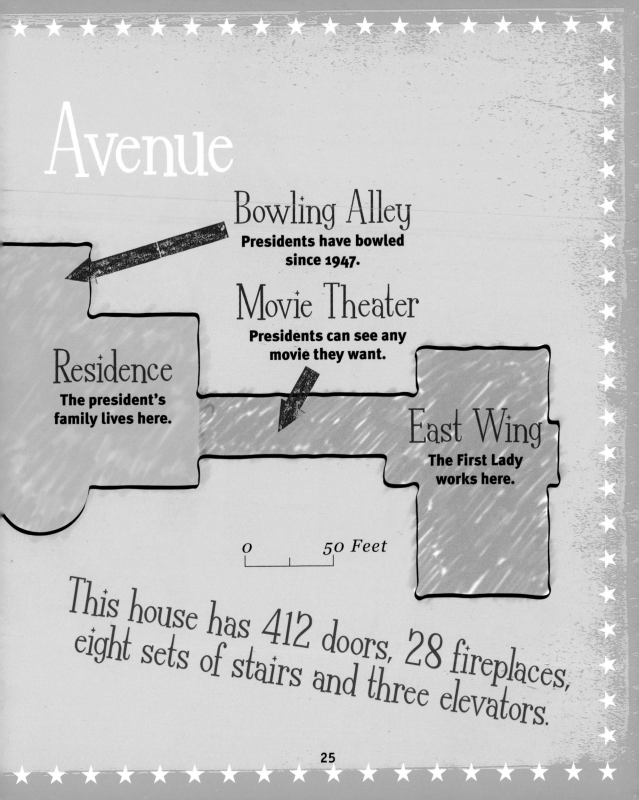

Avenue

Bowling Alley
Presidents have bowled since 1947.

Movie Theater
Presidents can see any movie they want.

Residence
The president's family lives here.

East Wing
The First Lady works here.

0   50 Feet

This house has 412 doors, 28 fireplaces, eight sets of stairs and three elevators.

President Lincoln gave a speech called the Gettysburg Address to dedicate a cemetery after the U.S. Civil War. This speech was only 10 sentences and 272 words long! Many people think it is one of the best speeches ever made in this country.

CHAPTER 5

Leading the Country Through Crises

" . . . government of the people, by the people, for the people, shall not perish from the earth."

—*Abraham Lincoln's Gettysburg Address*

In 1861, the United States fell apart. Eleven Southern states broke away from the rest of the country. These states formed a separate country called the Confederate States of America. Why did they do this?

The country was split over slavery and states' rights. Most Northern states wanted to stop slavery. Southern states wanted to keep it. They said the national government had no right to change state laws. Eleven states **seceded** from the Union on April 12, 1861, starting the Civil War.

Abraham Lincoln was president during this troubled time in the nation's history. The North won the war in 1865, but many people died.

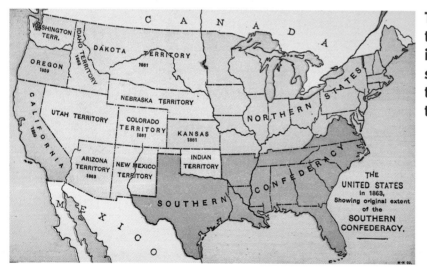

This is a map of the United States in 1863. The green states are the ones that seceded from the Union.

The Union's victory in the Civil War resulted in the freedom of almost 4 million African American slaves.

After the war, Lincoln wanted to make the country whole again. He said the Southern states could rejoin the Union in return for three things. They must promise to be loyal to the United States. They must promise to support the Constitution and U.S. laws. They must accept the end of slavery.

Lincoln's plan worked. It brought the country together and ended slavery. But he never lived to see it happen. On April 14, 1865, Lincoln was shot while watching a play at Ford's Theatre in Washington, D.C. He died the next day.

Roosevelt and the Great Depression

During the 1930s, the country endured the Great Depression. This was a long period of economic trouble. People could not find jobs.

In 1932, the voters elected Franklin D. Roosevelt. Roosevelt was confident and inspired people. His theme song was "Happy Days Are Here Again."

During the Great Depression, as many as 25 percent of people in the United States were unemployed. Many families were forced to travel throughout the country looking for work, shelter, and food.

Franklin D. Roosevelt was elected for four terms, but presidents today can serve only two.

In this radio broadcast in 1938, Roosevelt speaks to the nation from his home in Hyde Park, New York.

Roosevelt promised people a "New Deal." The New Deal was a series of laws to help people who were hurt by the Depression. One law created Social Security to pay people who are retired, unemployed, or disabled. Other programs hired people to build dams, roads, and bridges.

Roosevelt convinced Americans that the government was doing its best to help them through a terrible situation. He gave people hope.

Bush and September 11

On September 11, 2001, terrorists took control of four airplanes. They flew two of the planes into the Twin Towers of the World Trade Center in New York City. The 110-story buildings fell later that morning. The terrorists flew the third plane into the Pentagon, the headquarters of the Department of Defense, near Washington, D.C. Passengers tried to overpower terrorists on the fourth plane. It crashed in Pennsylvania.

Hijacked American Airlines Flight 77 crashed into the Pentagon on September 11, 2001.

President George W. Bush visited the devastation of the September 11 attacks on the World Trade Center.

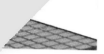

Nearly 3,000 people died, and many more were injured in the September 11 attacks. People across the country and around the world were in shock and worried about more attacks.

Leaders Through Crises

1861–1865
Abraham Lincoln
The Northern and Southern states clash in the Civil War.

1917–1918
Woodrow Wilson
The United States joins the fight in World War I.

President Bush worked hard to protect the country. He closed airports and sent National Guard troops to cities. He also established the Department of Homeland Security. This department is responsible for keeping Americans safe at home.

1929–1940
Herbert Hoover and
Franklin Delano Roosevelt
The Great Depression takes place.

1941–1945
Franklin Delano Roosevelt
and Harry S. Truman
**The United States fights
in World War II.**

2001
George W. Bush
**Terrorists carry out attacks on
New York City and Washington, D.C.**

The president flies in one of two 747 jets each called Air Force One. In this photo from 1988, Vice President George H. W. Bush speaks at a press conference in front of Air Force One. Behind him are (left to right) Barbara Bush, President Ronald Reagan, and First Lady Nancy Reagan.

CHAPTER 6

One Tough Job

What are the two most common nonpolitical careers held by former presidents prior to being elected? Lawyer — and farmer!

Being president is hard work. Usually every minute of a president's day is planned. Presidents speak to other world leaders. They meet with their staff and attend events. They speak to the press. They travel regularly to places near and far.

Air Force One has an office, several sleeping areas, and six bathrooms. Here, President Nixon (far right) is speaking with leaders about the conflict in Vietnam in 1969.

A Day in the Life of a President

What does a president do all day? Here's how a typical day might look.

5:30 A.M.   The day begins. The president eats breakfast, exercises, and reads newspapers.

7:00   The president takes the elevator down to the ground floor of the White House. He walks across the Rose Garden and enters the Oval Office. He begins meetings with his staff.

9:15   The national security adviser tells the president about situations around the world that affect U.S. security. Most of the information talked about in this meeting is top secret.

President Bush passes by the White House Rose Garden on his way to the Oval Office.

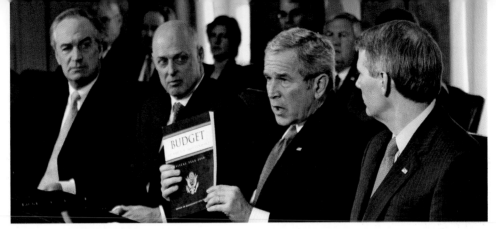

The president talks with his cabinet about many issues, including the national budget. Here, President Bush proposes a new budget for 2008 at his budget meeting.

10:00   The budget meeting begins. The president, the treasury secretary, and other officials talk about the country's annual budget.

12:30 P.M.   The president lunches in the White House dining room with some of the nation's top teachers. The teachers share their thoughts on educational issues.

2:00   The president calls the British prime minister. They discuss military issues that concern both countries.

4:00   The president signs a **bill** in the East Room of the White House. Once the bill is signed, it becomes law. He is joined by the group of teachers from lunch and students from different states. The senators and representatives who wrote the bill are there. The president uses a series of pens to sign the bill. He hands the pens out to the students and teachers as souvenirs.

5:30   The president goes upstairs to the family living area. Later, he dines with the first lady and the secretary of state.

8:00   The president and first lady watch a movie in the White House theater.

10:30   The president works in his private study for an hour or two before going to bed.

Protecting
the President

Secret Service agents give around-the-clock protection to the president and his family, the vice president, and past presidents.

The agents always travel with the president. A group of agents, called the advance team, goes to a city before a president's visit. Agents meet with local police. They make a plan to keep the president safe.

New agents go to a special school near Washington, D.C. They learn how to protect a president, and themselves, in an emergency.

A Rewarding Challenge

Every day is a little different from the previous one when you're the president. But each day is likely to be filled with challenges. So why do people want this job? The people who run for president are proud to be Americans. They are willing to put in long hours for their country. To them, the hard work is a sacrifice worth making. ★

President John F. Kennedy reaches out to shake hands with his supporters.

Requirements to be president: At least 35 years old, born in the United States, and a U.S. resident for at least 14 years, and a U.S. citizen

Length of one term: 4 years

First U.S. president: George Washington

Location of the president's office: Oval Office in the White House in Washington, D.C.

First president to live in the White House: John Adams, in 1800

Number of presidents from 1789 to 2008: 43

Only president elected to four terms: Franklin D. Roosevelt, served from 1933 to 1945

Youngest to take office: Theodore Roosevelt, 42

Oldest to take office: Ronald Reagan, 69

Did you find the truth?

T George Washington got paid nothing for being president.

F The Constitution gives the president unlimited power.

Resources

Books

Adams, Simon. *The Presidents of the United States*. Minnetonka, MN: Two-Can, 2005.

Davis, Kenneth C. *Don't Know Much About the Presidents*. New York: Harper Trophy, 2003.

Davis, Todd, and Mark Frey. *The New Big Book of U.S. Presidents*. Philadelphia: Courage Books, 2005.

January, Brendan. *Air Force One*. Danbury, CT: Children's Press, 2004.

January, Brendan. *The Presidency*. Danbury, CT: Children's Press, 2004.

Santella, Andrew. *U.S. Presidential Inaugurations*. Danbury, CT: Children's Press, 2002.

St. George, Judith. *So You Want to Be President?* New York: Philomel, 2004.

Taylor-Butler, Christine. *The Constitution*. Danbury, CT: Children's Press, 2008.

Organizations and Web Sites

The National Archives: Presidential Libraries

www.archives.gov/presidential-libraries/

Find out more about the country's presidential libraries.

PBS Kids: "The Democracy Project"

pbskids.org/democracy/

Check out this site to be president for a day!

The White House Historical Association

www.whitehousehistory.org

Take a virtual tour of the White House.

The White House Kids Page

www.whitehousekids.gov

Find out the latest White House news, and watch videos of presidential pets.

Places to Visit

The White House

1600 Pennsylvania Avenue NW
Washington, D.C. 20500
202-456-1414
www.whitehouse.gov

Important Words

bill – a written plan of a new law

cabinet – the group of senior officials who advise the head of state

executive (ig-ZE-kyuh-tiv) – related to the branch of government that enforces laws; the president is part of the executive branch

federal – relating to a form of government in which states are united under one central power

foreign policy (FOR-uhn PAW-luh-see) – plans that a government follows when dealing with other countries

impeach – to bring charges against a public official for a crime

inauguration (i-NAW-gyuh-RAY-shuhn) – a formal ceremony to place someone in an official position

oath of office – the formal promise of a public official to perform the duties of a job faithfully

Revolutionary War – the war from 1775 to 1783 that gave the 13 American colonies independence from Great Britain, forming the United States of America

seceded (si-SEED-ed) – formally withdrew from a group

term – the set length of time an elected official serves in office

veto (VEE-toh) – a refusal to approve a legislative bill

Index

About the Author

Christine Taylor-Butler has written more than 30 books for children. She has written several books in the True Book American History series, including *The Bill of Rights*, *The Constitution*, *The Congress of the United States*, *The Supreme Court*, and *Explorers of North America*.

A native of Ohio, Taylor-Butler now lives in Kansas City, Missouri, with her husband, Ken, and their two daughters. She holds degrees in both civil engineering and art and design from the Massachusetts Institute of Technology.